Also by the author

Poetry
Snakeskin Stilettos
Beneath the Ice
The Horse's Nest

MIRACLE FRUIT

MIRACLE FRUIT

MOYRA DONALDSON

LAGAN PRESS
BELFAST
2010

Acknowledgements
Versions of some of these poems have previously appeared in *The SHOp*, *Poetry Ireland Review*, *The Tatler* and *West 47*.

The author also wishes to acknowledge the support of the Arts Council of Northern Ireland for an Individual Artist Award in 2009, which enabled the completion of this collection.

Published by
Lagan Press
Unit 45
Westlink Enterprise Centre
30-50 Distillery Street
Belfast BT12 5BJ
e-mail: lagan-press@e-books.org.uk
web: lagan-press.org.uk

ARTS
COUNCIL
of Northern Ireland

ISBN: 978 1 904652 98 4 (pbk)
978 1 904652 99 1 (hbk)
Author: Donaldson, Moyra
Title: Miracle Fruit
2010

for John, Claire and Jannah

Contents

DAVE SAYS IT MUST HAVE BEEN
A HUMMINGBIRD HAWK MOTH

Home from work, it's hot; summer of '06. Getting out of the car I see a tiny hummingbird hovering at the mouth of a blossom. I'm watching it drink, watching the blur of its wings, astounded that I have brought this into my garden when the robin that lives in the holly tree, flies out and swallows it.

I have witnessed the beginning of the end of the universe.

HUNTER

"Ah!" said Sipsop, "I only wish Jack [Hunter] Tearguts had had the cutting of Plutarch. He understands anatomy better than any of the Ancients. He'll plunge his knife up to the hilt in a single drive, and thrust his fist in, and all in the space of a quarter of an hour. He does not mind their crying, tho' they cry ever so. He'll swear at them & keep them down with his fist, & tell them that he'll scrape their bones if they don't lay still & be quiet. What the devil should the people in the hospital that have it done for nothing, make such a piece of work for? ... & we think you think we are are rascals. I do as I chuse. What is it to any body what I do? I am always unhappy too. When I think of Surgery—I don't know. I do it because I like it. .

— William Blake, 'Island in the Moon'

WHAT JOHN HUNTER SAID TO ME

January 2010

You know I lived
in a world of pain:
everyone did.
The best surgeon
was the fastest surgeon,
and I was the fastest:

and the hungriest.
Whatever was strange
in nature I wanted it.
Try it. Take it apart.
Explain it. Know it.
No boundaries restrained me.
I was the most excellent.

I could fill the steep raked
benches of St Thomas's hospital
with gentlemen in broadcloth coats
and powdered wigs; they leant
on their gold topped canes,
straining forward to hear me lecture,
of the mercury and sweating cure
for venereal disease,
or the transplantation of teeth.

I could stand for hours in the cold,
my only company the opened stinking corpse
before me, and I myself almost motionless,
a pair of forceps and my own open fingers,
picking asunder the connecting fibres
of structure, the heart, the lactating breast,

the organs of reproduction; patient as a prophet,
sure that truth would come and darkness become light.

All the death that passed through my workshop —
human, animal — enabled my vast understanding
of comparative anatomy, of all flesh,

so I could slice fearlessly through life,
remove a leg shattered by gunshot, or fingers
crushed beneath a wheel, or a cancerous breast.
I could crack a chest to repair an aortic aneurism.
By what authority do you judge me? Do you not also
want your surgeon to know his job, to cut well?

THE SKELETON OF THE GREAT IRISH GIANT

I

Conceived on the very top
of a very high haystack,
in Little Bridge, Co Derry,
by his stout, strong voiced mother
and his average sized father,
Charles Byrne grew like a corn stalk
and was the talk of London
for years: could be seen
at the sign of the Hampshire
Hog for half a crown,
or one shilling for children
and servants in livery.
He too had a voice that sounded
like thunder, but his appearance
was far from wholesome.
He constantly dribbled and spat.

Out of fashion,
his savings stolen,
his limbs always aching
and his drinking
killing him surely,
the surgeons gathered
around the house
where he lay
like harpooners
round a whale.
How he feared
their hunger for him.

When he died,
the fishermen
he had employed
to sink his leaded body
twenty fathoms down
and out of reach,
succumbed to the bribes.
Handed the huge corpse over
for five hundred pounds.

In his Earl's Court
menagerie, laboratory,
John Hunter, foremost
of those surgeons
and a true scientist,
cut the Irish Giant

into chunks and boiled him
in a great copper kettle.
Water plumping, he kept
the Irish Giant bubbling
and simmering for days,
fat skimmed off the top:
prepared the skeleton to hang
in his own famous Museum.

Disappointingly, the hung frame,
the articulated bones,
measured in at only seven feet
and seven inches, not the eight
feet four the Irish Giant
and his manager
had (fraudulently) claimed
and furthermore

he wasn't the last of his kind.
There was the other Irish Giant
and the Gigantic Twin Brothers
who were also natives of Ireland.
Still, his skeleton was a popular exhibit
in the Hunterian and remains there,
an impressive sight even to this day.

II

What? Bones can't speak.
We are all dumb here
in Mr Hunter's marvellous collection
of morbid anatomy, curiosities
and human misery.
Silent as the grave, we hang or float
in our limbo of glass cases
and jars of formaldehyde, darkness
forbidden to us, constantly on show.
We are the blunt truths of the flesh;
what further story do you expect
from me or my twisted companion
bought for eighty five guineas,
Mr Jaffs, with his fibrodysplasia
ossificans progressiva;

or from all the unnamed,
the sliced and the hacked,
from the part of the face
of a child with small pox,
from the penis and bladder
of a small boy, the skull
of an old woman
who has lost all her teeth,
the breast with a large carcinoma,

the rectum with haemorrhoids,
the femur fractured by gunshot,
the foetuses, the vagina, the femoral artery.
Expendable, all of us, voiceless in death
as in life, we serve to illustrate. What?

MRS FRAME

A Horse-Courser's Wife,
lately living in Barbican,
was afflicted with a swelling
for which she was tapt
and at two tappings
had sixteen gallons of water
let out of her.

She thought — when the Disease
first came upon her
about eleven years ago —
that she was with child
and would not be persuaded
to the contrary ever since.

Just before she died
at St Bartholomew's Hospital,
she earnestly desired to be opened
and accordingly, when the Surgeons
had made an incision of her womb,
they found therein the skeleton of a child,
the bones whereof were knitted all together
in their due proportion, but all the flesh thereof
perished and consumed by its emersion in so much water.

NOTES TAKEN IN THE HUNTERIAN

— the Animals – 24ʰ October 2009

'John Hunter takes in everything'
Peter Camper, Dutch anatomist

disturbing and random
no interest in taxonomy

network of collectors
former students
travellers naturalists
naval officers
merchants of trading companies

copper boiler in an outhouse

tours for ladies and gentlemen

intestine of a pelican
colon of a lion
fallopian tube of a bottle nosed whale
foetus of a rhesus monkey
hand and head of a young chimp
'half beast half human'

humerus of a swan
vagina of a minke whale
tip of an elephant's tongue
lower jaw of a golden eagle
brain of a crocodile
from a private menagerie

a grey seal's nose
liver of an opossum
liver of a camel
ovaries of a Surinam toad
a large pregnant African scorpion

and on and on
including the results
of the experimental transplant
of a human tooth
into a cockerel's comb

all the product of his
'virtuous labour'
demonstrating
his 'genius and ardent zeal'

THE SOW-GELDER

He was in the company of several other married men
over a pot or two of ale, when they all joined
in complaint of the fruitfulness of their wives, and asked
could he not spay their wives as he did other animals.
He said he could, and they all agreed their good women
should undergo the operation, provided he would begin
with his own. This with a great oath he undertook.

At home, by violence he bound and gagged his wife
and laying her on the table, made a transverse incision
on the side of her belly, but after much puzzling,
he found there was some difference between the situation
of the parts in the rational and irrational animals, and so,
sewing up the wound, he was forced to give up the experiment.

At the late Assizes held in Bridgewater,
his wife refused to prosecute,
acknowledged her forgiveness of him,
and desired the court would do the same.

BONE VOICES — EARL'S COURT

We are a very minor pit of bones;
a pit of very minor bones: the poor,
the won't be missed,

tinker, tailor, soldier,
beggar woman, thief,
the pregnant servant girl
who swallowed arsenic,

brought by cart for burial
from the dissecting room
in Castle Street,
delivered at night
through the iron gate
and the drawbridge
that allows access
to the underground yard
of Jack Tearguts.

We know there are pits of bones
everywhere, everywhere
bones and bones and bones,

metacarpals, vertebrae, empty
ribs and skulls that once were
women, children, men,

we taste their numbers
and their silence
in the earth, in the particles

of dirt that pack our jaws.
None of us have any say
in the matter: never have.

AN EXPERIMENT ON
A BIRD IN AN AIR PUMP

painting by Joseph Wright of Derby

Hyper-realistic eighteenth century light, falling
especially to make a point, illuminate a profile;
light that insistently contradicts the darkness,

ranging emotions set out in faces, witnesses
to the birth of science, that precocious, cruel,
self regarding child with the expendable
dying bird, white cockatoo, exotic marker
of discovery; suffocating, forewarning.

OLD GODS IN THE BRITISH MUSEUM

They don't cope well
all cooped up together,
so many different persuasions
rubbing shoulders under the one roof.

All uprooted, un-worshipped,
held impotent in cold Albion,
fed only the thinnest gruel of awe
from tourists with cameras.

Beneath the impassivity
of their stone faces, they seethe,
or weep, or mutter: some have forgotten
altogether what it was to be feared.

FAMILIAR

So strange and beautiful
little mummified falcon,
all wrapped up and lain
in the corner of the display case.

I watch you wheel in the sky
that is the same sky, beneath
the sun that is the same sun,
your wings lean on the wind,

and it is as if I have always
known you on my wrist and you
have hunted for me in that life
as you will hunt for me in the next.

PORTALS

I fell across the doorway, golden heights went on forever,
Anubis weighed my soul as not lighter than a feather.

I fell across the doorway into the open mouth of harm,
the leaves, the leaves all whispering of the approaching storm.

I fell across the doorway, every thing was black and red,
the Prince of the Lilies picked me up, carried me to bed.

CRAZY DAISY

Our thin nosed collie who saw visions in the air
and was mad as a god, tapped with her paw
at our living room window the night after she died,
as she always did when she wanted in: we heard,
but couldn't find the door that would admit her.

BECOMING AN ASCETIC

It was Diogenes the Cynic who suggested it to me,
the barrel; showed me the very one, a wine cask,
oak and iron, made by a skilled cooper, a thing
of beauty in itself and capable of holding me.

I climb down inside, crouch; the curve fits my spine
perfectly, my legs a tent, knees against my chest.
When I lift my head, stretch my neck back
and look up, I see that stars in daylight also shine.

THE YEAR OF THE GREAT WINTER

Nearly all the birds died.
Fish froze in the rivers,
animals froze in the forests.
Trees exploded and game
lay down in the fields and died.

Wine froze in the barrels
and it took an axe to cut the bread.

Breath was transformed
into a shower of ice crystals,
falling from mouths
with a tinkling sound,
like the whispers of stars.

HOW TO FEED YOUR LOVER

Starter – Ortolan

First catch your songbird, blind it,
force feed it millet, grapes and figs,
then drown the tiny creature in Armagnac,
de-feather and roast for a few minutes
in its own juices: place the embroidered
napkin over your lover's head, to shield her
from the gaze of God and serve her
this two ounces of life, place it hot
on her tongue, only the beak protruding
from her lips: the aromas will fill her senses.
See if she can taste the entire life of the bird,
and, fixed between the last air and the Armagnac,
the flavour of guilt, see if she can cease to exist
except as taste itself, as the small bones lacerate
her gums, as she bites down and chews,
her own blood mixing with the bird's flesh.

Main Course – Blowfish

Buy your fish from the market
where they are sold alive
with their mouths stitched shut.
Slice the flesh thinly, and tenderly
prepare a fine dish of sashimi.
The fish's skin can be puffed up
with air and used as a lantern
for gentle illumination of the feast,
then see if she will trust you enough
to eat; that even when her lips begin

35

to tingle and become numb,
she'll trust you have not served up
the poison to which there is no antidote.

Dessert – Miracle Fruit

This may prove difficult to source,
you may need to send to the ends
of the earth: but all that is needed
is just a sliver of this mythic fruit.
It is well worth the expense and effort,
for once she has eaten it, you will
forever taste of violets in her mouth.

HOW TO BECOME A BUDDHA
THROUGH SELF- MUMMIFICATION

These instructions are not intended for the young,
indeed to take this route whilst in the prime of life
would merely show an excessive obsession
with the physical world
and do you no good at all,
but when you start to feel your strength begin to fade
and know your days are numbered anyway,
here is how you can begin to disregard your life
yet also leave behind an artefact of your struggle.

For the first one thousand days, eat nothing but nuts,
walnuts, hazelnuts; and seeds, sunflower and pumpkin,
there is no particular prescriptive listing, but you must also
subject yourself to severe physical hardship and exercise.
This regime will remove most body fat, leaving nothing
that will easily putrefy.

For the next one thousand days
drink tea made from the bark and roots of the urushi tree,
that same tree from which lacquer is made for furniture.
This will induce vomiting, sweating, urination,
further dehydrating your body so you will be a living skeleton.
The poison in your system will kill the maggots and insects
that will want to feed on your corpse in the tomb.
Take only from the sacred spring, whose arsenic laden waters
will preserve whatever meat is still left on the bone.

Next is the entombment, a stone tomb, where there is just
enough space for you to assume the lotus position.
There will be a tube for air, and a small bell.

You will ring the bell every day, and when the bell stops ringing,
the tomb will be sealed.

When another thousand days have passed,
someone will open the tomb.
If your body has mummified, you are a Buddha
and your remains will be displayed with honour.
If your body has decomposed, you have not
attained nirvana this time around: your tomb
will be resealed and you will find yourself reborn.

AMYGDALA

The crocodile in my brain grins,
my tears are crocodile tears.
Sobek and me will never go hungry:
one hundred million choices every year.

THE OPENING OF THE MOUTH CEREMONY

Seventy days after death, begin the ritual,
place my body in a standing position,
facing south, have a close member of my family
burn incense: the women should wail
and priests attend, foremost
the jackal-masked impersonator of Anubis,
and Ptah, skullcapped dwarf god
who brought all things into being
by thinking of them and saying them with his tongue.

Place my possessions in the tomb —
my bed, my favourite chair and my laptop,
my clothes, jewellery, make-up and perfume,
the foreleg of a sacrificial calf, spurting fresh blood.

Then chant the potent spells, touch my lips with the adze,
metal of heaven that has split open the mouths of the gods.

*

Present me to the child who loves me, who will touch
my mouth with her little finger, as at birth her mouth
was cleaned: so I will have life in the hereafter.

MY WANDERING WOMB

I stand up
it climbs the ladder of my spine, lodges
itself at the base of my brain.

I lie down
it crawls along my windpipe to crouch
at the back of my throat —

such vagrancy!

Like an animal within an animal
it is altogether erratic: is it any wonder
that I feel panicky, slightly hysterical even?

WILLIAM WALKER

Diver's Work Saves a Great Cathedral
*Famous Winchester Edifice
is Preserved from Destruction*
New York Times, 28 July, 1912

Brass helmet, canvas suit, wing nuts
screwed tight, chest, back and boots
weighted with lead, airline attached,
and six hours of every twenty four
the pump's rhythm draws pushes
air in out, my lungs expand, contract.

I love the sound, the hiss and thump:
it's where I live, at God's foundations,
and though I cannot see, I feel my way
to what's correct, where each block fits.
One hundred and fifteen thousand blocks,
nine hundred thousand bricks, six years
in the singular moment of breath and task –
the treasure that I dive to find.

THE FIRST HUNTERIAN ORATION 1814
— JOHN ABERNETHY

In celebration of and with respect for John Hunter,
my old anatomy teacher, who like many men of science
had turned his thoughts towards mysticism
when approaching the end of his days,
my lecture was entitled *An Enquiry into the Probability
and Rationality of Mr Hunter's Theory of Life*.

After his death I had found, among his chaotic,
bloodstained papers, several manuscripts in which
he laid out his theories of a life force, or principle,
associated with the spontaneous motions inherent
in human physiology: systolic and diastolic pulses
of the heart, male erection and female blushing.

He came to the conclusion that blood
held the secret of Vitality and I like to believe
he also came to see God in the blood.
I built upon his speculations, drawing an analogy
between Vitality and Electricity, calling on the authority
of Mr Humphry Davy's lectures at the Royal Society.
I brought scientific evidence — if not exactly
proof — to the theological notion of the soul. Electricity
as a metaphor for life itself. A super added force,
ergo some force outside of man has added it.

My most scathing critic was my fellow Professor of Anatomy,
William Lawrence, who had also been my youngest
and most gifted pupil. He holds a more materialist view
of human life and has little time for conventional pieties,
but still it was an unexpected blow from my young protégé

who had been my assistant since he was sixteen
and had lodged for three years with me and my wife.

I am a plain speaking man, a Calvinist, I do not hesitate
to tell even my richest and most famous clients what I think,
to diagnose as I see it, Coleridge for example, despite
all his complex symptoms — a simple case of opium addiction;
still I could not help but feel bitter about Lawrence's betrayal
of me, a little allegiance to his teacher behoves a man well.

So I saw it as my duty when he started his own lectures,
to ridicule his materialism and his assertions that mental
processes, thoughts and consciousness are a function
of the brain: this is an undermining of the moral welfare
of the people. The subsequent storm of disapproval
for his atheism is a comfort to me; like Lord Byron
he is labelled a revolutionary, his lectures are ruled
blasphemous and he is persecuted and may be prosecuted.
He is forced to withdraw his book the *Natural History of Man*.

MONSTER

Hot lightning bolt
that liquefies, rises
through the base
chakra, to the heart
chakra, crown chakra,
and the creature
opens her eyes,
awakes again.

She raises her hand,
touches her face,
her throat, the neat
line of sutures
where he has stitched
her soul back
into her voice;
dear surgeon,

but dazed as she is,
already she fears
the moment when
he will step from
the taxi into
the midnight street
and leave her.
She has seen
the movie:
when the mob
surround her,
and he has gone,
how will she
remember who she is?

DEEP SPACE AND CAROLINE

When I was a small child, my father
showed me an eclipse of the sun
in a bucket of water.
I would lie awake at night
listening to my brothers
Jacob and William arguing,
over Leibniz and Newton
and the new mathematics
of gradients and curves.

I felt the aftershock
from the Lisbon earthquake
when I was five,
and felt it once more
when I was seventeen, stood
by my father's deathbed.

My face scarred by smallpox,
my growth stunted from typhus,
my destiny was to be the housekeeper,
the spinster, the family's maid

but I wore a gag to learn to sing

and at twenty one I watched constellations
from the top of a postchaise, moving
across Europe, accompanied
by my beloved brother William
and by the rhythm of horses' hooves
and the beat beat beat of my heart
escaping.

*

I will learn English.
I will run a milliner's shop
and host William's salons.
I will sing for our supper.
I will be full of dreams
and longings.

I will help in the grinding
of the mirrors, sometimes
sixteen hours at a stretch
in the stone flagged basement
among the tools and chemicals
and the horse dung moulds.
I will keep my brother nourished
by placing the food into his mouth.
I will read to him, relieveing the tedium
of the polishing that cannot stop
lest the metal mist, become useless.
I will be his 'boy', his assistant.

I will sit with him and take notes
of his all night stellar measurements
and observations, together
we will mind the heavens.

I will practise seeing for myself

and with my hunter's telescope
I will sweep the skies
methodically
and find my comet.

I will fall into the night
where there is nothing
to save us
from knowing
our infinite smallness.

I will destroy all my journals
that speak of personal things.

UNQUIET

As I was going up the stair,
I met a man who wasn't there.

—W.H. Mearns

STRANG-FIORD

A man in the bar says he's seen five dead foxes
on the road to Downpatrick in the last week.

There is a strong tide running.
Where the red flowers grow
on the wall and in the spaces
between years it is not safe;
even the horse and rider
do not see the harbour,
but look inwards
to the blue bed after-
noon and the portrait self.
The hallway groans with ghosts
who pass each other on the stairs,
coming and going, coming and going,
while behind the wall the ox- eye daisies
have come back: the gooseberries are ripe.

I am a wagered coin, a silver shilling,
tossed and spinning, falling, heads or tails.

UNQUIET

For months I've wandered with the dead
through the mansions of their father's house
or across the flat landscape of the underworld.

The dead are not happy, but neither are they
truly unhappy, sad more than anything;
his kiss is a question unanswered,

she has resolved nothing. I want my own
dreams back, the high desert, the green growing,
the whole chaotic caboodle of my life.

PORTRAIT OF MY BROTHER
AS AN OX-BOW LAKE

Water that has forgotten the flow

that now turns in on itself

choked

still

cut off from me

only visible over my shoulder

HUNGER

The year is starting to turn round again,
dark afternoons creeping a little towards
the light, and birds are venturing out;
the mistle thrush, his chest still narrow
with winter, wings from tree to sluggy
ground with adolescent bravado: in the
holly bush, the robin who last summer
swallowed the universe, uncoils it from
his throat. The starved horse is starting
to round out again at last, sharp angle
of bones softening as flesh creeps back.
She doesn't lift her head from cropping
grass with teeth made long by hunger,
moving only to find the next, the next bite.

MEMENTO

Here: let me give you this crumpled dress,
this rainy night, this moth cocoon,
the voice on the other end of the phone.

Take this small misunderstanding,
this word not spoken, the touch withheld
and the touch given, the hawk's wing.

Have them, the grains of sand,
the full blown rose, the horse's footfall
and the candlelight, this book of rules;

all strung together, necklaced around
your throat, remembrance, fastened
by a smooth white stone, a twist of hair.

DUNLUCE AVENUE

At each evening's return
you hold the key ready,
push the light switch in
and race the timer two flights
to your bedsit before the hall
and stairs are taken over again
by darkness. This is a house
of dingy melancholy, you're
spooked by it, wish you'd
never moved here, you're
lonely here; it's all wrong.

Be reassured, thirty years from now,
you will have forgotten most things
about this place; no memory
remaining of furniture, décor,
the particular fear

but you will remember
the professor of Japanese,
elderly and rumpled, soft
as a feather pillow and sad
as a lost empire: his footsteps
across the floor above
in the long hours before dawn.
How you used to wait
for the knock on your door.
Open it, he will be there
holding a jar of warm sake.

A WOMAN ADDRESSES HER BODY

For all my talk of soul, it was you
always, sweet little beast, amoral
animal, who showed me the ways
of Love, its passions and crucifixions.

The artist, the anatomist, the poet
and the surgeon, they have seen
the glory in you; you beatified them
in the moments where they believed.

You are my way, my truth, my life,
I am what you have made of me
and still I do not know the limits of you,
or where you will take me next.

BARR HALL

1

This shoreline's stones hold information
in the lines that run and angle through them,
in the circles and swirls: soft through hard,
laid down by time, translated by the sea,
encrypted by tides and fractals of erosion.

What manner of man: when he asked for bread?
I keep my eyes down among the stones, sure
that if I look well enough, I'll find the one
that holds the message for me, understand
what's written there, as it was in the child's eyes.

2

After three days it's getting that I feel I nearly
know this house. I know where the dead spider is,
I know how to draw the blinds, how to lock the door
and the quality of the mornings: I know how to lie awake.

I've never heard the sound of seals before,
the bluster, cough and wet rasp of their voices.
I watch the tall masted ship cross the Barr
and it does not feel as if everything I notice
has been noticed before, though the seagulls
mock that thought, raucous as drunks.

I have been too anxious, running after meaning:
let the images dance where circumferences touch,
where the overlap occurs, where the meteors
shower down like golden coins burning through blue
before being extinguished in the hissing waves.

3

Among the calls of gulls and curlews,
where mullet mill in the shallows
and my feet have a rhythm on the stones,
I am peaceful and at ease.

The distant constant Mournes,
the peninsula with its familiar litany
of names, townlands and villages:
Ballywhiskin, Kircubbin, Glastry,

Cardy, Ballywalter, Ards,
cartography of my childhood, of my life.
This is my home, this small acreage
and for the first time, I feel at home

now that so much has dropped away
and I want less and I want more.
A colder madness holds me in the stillness
of Cuan my lough of safe haven.

ALONE

If I lived by myself
I would be careful about things,
I wouldn't burn to death
because of the candle
forgotten.

I'd get more sleep,
my washing would
always be done
and my correspondence
up to date.

I'm not sure how much I would drink
or smoke,
it could be less
or it could be more.
I'd eat better.

GLADIOLI

How glad I am that months ago, I planted
the bulbs whose growth I harvest now
against our too early, low skied autumn.

Lustful, affirmative, they move this evening
to a different place just by being on the window sill
in their white vase, the evening blue behind them.

Vigorous spears, I hear their colour behind my eyes,
jubilant life, rebounding off the bone, bouncing
chamber to chamber and on through every artery and vein.

SLIEVEMOYLE LOVE POEM

Like a painting you might buy,
it is a beautiful raw morning, a dark-
lit dawn after a night of love's déjà vu;
of winter storming around the stone walls,
and my not discomforting dreams of a thin
grey long-nosed dog and green Venetian islands.

Death is twice over
poking his long nose
into my life again,
and I'm tired of him
the proud old bastard

always leaving loose ends
always either too soon
or too late

only the young
are half in love
with him.

I am in love
with the man
who believes
in life.

GRIEF

If I were to write
another poem
about grief,
it would be full
of the absences
of animals —

Kitty, Dilly, Pip and Daisy,
Sezmo, Princess, Baby ...

each small loss
another lesson: every
thing we love will go away.

CLUTTER

I bring stones from beaches
and crystals from shops
that smell of incense; bowls
and candles, drinking vessels,
fossils from eons ago, fossils
from childhood; masks,
flowers and plants, lacquered
boxes, boxes of stone, books,
and gods of all persuasions,
Buddha, Ganesh, Anubis.

You bring flints and hides
and newspapers and parts
of old computers; updated
software and non fictional
accounts of heroes; balances,
antlers, Tibetan artefacts,
horns that called to prayer
and pieces of obsolete
scientific instruments.

Every surface congested,
every drawer stuffed full,
random objects, things
and bits of things
that might be useful someday.
Yet some days,
it is still the absences we feel.

31ST JANUARY

I want to be somewhere
else; out of this greyness
and in amongst heat, colour;
orange, olive, terracotta, red,
where even the yellow stone
is warm from holding the sun

and only the white marble,
quarried from darkness
is cool, and just the right
coolness against my skin,
my skin that tingles with
heat and light full of gold,

where even the night is warm
and scented with lemon
and I will sit outside,
supper on bread and olives,
apricots and walnuts, stars,
bare arms and summer's wine.

ADVICE WRITTEN ON THE OCCASION
OF A FRIEND'S FIFTIETH BIRTHDAY

Harden your heart, don't try to work out
who was wrong and who was right. Take
your pleasure where you can find it. Say
little and do not let anyone know what
you really think. If you don't like someone
stay away from them. Owe nothing, don't
concern yourself with understanding your
self, it serves no useful purpose, have no
animals, when they die you will just get
upset. Regard everyone with suspicion, take
nothing for granted, not even the evidence
of your own eyes. Do not talk to the dead,
particularly those who visit in dreams, they
rarely tell the truth and are too fond
of unnecessary symbolism. Remember
intuition is a useful tool, but is not infallible.
Don't join Facebook or play online bingo.
Nurture a liking for American cop series, and
don't worry if you weep at the most random
of things, keep up appearances when you go
out, it's amazing how a face can pull itself
together for a social occasion. Self-medicate.

BALANCES

It is the longest day,
the orange sunset on the black horizon balances
the orange moon rising through black clouds,
one horse is the shadow of the other, light
and dark are in my heart; I am equidistant
from north and south, east and west.
Three hundred and sixty degrees
I have surrounded myself with guardians:
gods and dragon dogs and multitudes of birds.
The wind still worries at me though,
it comes from all directions, changeable,
finding every crack in my defences,
laying low all manner of things, my rest,
my senses, my delicate blossoms —
I will plant only what can survive.

LEARNING THE WAY

The mice have their ways
through the house, along
the pipes, through the gaps
in floorboards,
to anywhere they want.

Listen,
at night
the mothers
leading the little ones
along the ways of the house

so that next year,
when the weather
turns cold, the new
generation will know
how to inhabit our space.

*

We've had enough of tiny teeth
gnawing through our dreams,
pellets of shit in the hot press,
incessant scratching behind the walls

so each night we set the traps
and each morning there is
a mother's body to be disposed of,
in the bin, neck snapped.

After a week, ten days,
the smell begins to sickly, sweetly
rise from under the floorboards,
from the nests, from the unfed dead pups.

BEEKEEPER

sends me a gift, a tiny cage
of silver filigree and bone,
scalpel carved,

inside the cage
a single honey bee,
buzzing with entrapment.

That night I dream
of a mossy bed, blue
bells, honey dripping

onto a veil, my mouth
stung, my lips swelling,
my voice gone.

DOUBT

The next day is stormy and the coast
has changed: silver light, silver waves.
His hair is silver, coarse like the pelt
of an animal, a seal lifting its wet head
through the sea: me on the wild shore.

How far away I feel, how forsaken
by the god I don't believe in: and by
this saviour that speaks in tongues
of fire and flesh and poetry, lying
as I lie, embraced in a worn out faith.

SOLAR LANTERNS

As night falls, they hold a vestige of the sun,
enough to shine among the garden's late green,
like candles lit for safe return : like the candles
I have lit in churches and cathedrals,
cities and towns I happen to be tourist in,
struck against my unbelief and for my dead.
Just little lights, not much against the dark.

CIRCUS

A tragic, self-serving procession of freaks, misfits, sad sacks …
—Times' columnist Martin Samuel
on the Jeremy Kyle Show

SINS OF THE FATHERS

A young woman of Galloway, having proved with child,
laid the same to a respectable man, John Woods by name.
This man denied having ever known the woman, said
he never would acknowledge that the child was his
unless his name was written at full length upon its face.
He gave his solemn oath before the court to that effect.

This wonderful child has now arrived in our city of Edinburgh
and been inspected by the Professors, who pronounced him
to be a most wonderful phenomenon and an astonishing
dispensation of Providence pointing out the truth.

I, Doctor Munro, invite you now to witness this wonder for
    yourselves,
for just a small fee, see the putative power of Maternal Impression,
the alleged father's name in legible letters in his infant son's
    right eye:
John Woods, who when he came to know this circumstance,
instantly absconded and has not been heard of since.

*

His father's name remained in my mind's eye
all the long months of my disgrace, I held
it there, a constant, as my belly swelled
and people turned their faces from me in the street.

When finally the midwife placed him in my arms,
bloody and squalling, I felt nothing, turned from him,
even when they told me it was written plain in his right eye,
his father's name and in the left, 1817, the year of his birth.

The plan to exhibit him was not mine,
but I haven't missed him, don't regret
my decision to let the doctor take him.
I get money sent to me each month.

MAN BEAR IN LONDON 1720

We have a very odd creature here,
like a man in shape,
but furred like a bear.
They tell us he came from Ireland,
where he lived till he was twenty
and ran wild in the woods.

All the parts of his body
are overgrown with long black hair,
which they have stiffened and rubbed backwards:
makes him look very deliciously it seems,
and the women go in shoals to see him.

They show him for two-pence a piece
and an innumerable many customers they have had;
but as they expose him no lower than his waist,
their trade begins to fail them,
and the females' curiosity to abate

MARY PATTERSON

Plied with gin, stupefied,
Burke's knee on my breast,
Hare's hand across my breath
'til the life is pressed out of me,
then I'm delivered to your door

and it was one thing Dr Knox,
who buys the beef,
to take my body
for professional
scientific purposes,
for the greater good
so to speak,

and for certain my body
was worth more as dead meat:
I'd hitch up my skirts
for just a few coins
in the shadows of Canongate,
whereas you paid seven pounds
and ten shillings,

but to lay me out like that,
naked on the couch,
sensuously arranged
under the flickering candlelight,
my dead face seductively
turned to the audience,
and a white sheet draped
teasingly over my calves

and then have me sketched
before my dissection

now that's a disgrace.
What were you thinking?

And you Mr Ferguson, surgeon
in training, looking at me,
in your professional capacity

as I looked at you in mine
just two nights previous.
You still want to use me.

HOGARTH SELF-PORTRAIT WITH PUG

Dublin 2007

Who is this and what is she doing here
like a distorting mirror, looking at me
as if I am not me but her; a different time,
but still with my pug beside me and still
gin lane, the four stages, the marriage à la

mode. I've been kind to myself, but she knows
how it is: outside it is raining and as the needle
disappears into the grey sky, the same things
are happening that have always happened,
and nothing is so black and white that it is

not lived in vividness. I'm only part of this,
and so is she, and those she's with, the figures
beside her, behind her, inside her, jostling,
casting a shadow backwards to what lies
before us all, and the whole line up of us

knows its about flesh, its influence, the demands
it makes upon us, its hungers and requirements;
how it makes us who we are, despite our desire
to be something lighter: it holds us to ourselves.
Ballast to our souls, vain blood looks through.

BALLOON

What an absolutely wonderful day.
I was dressed of course for the occasion,
a new dress, the bodice cut low
to show my magnificent breasts
to best advantage,
and the silk, a deep red
to complement
the swags of heavier silk
that draped the wicker gondola.

So in we clambered, Mr Lunardi,
young Mr Biggin the Old Etonian,
and me — Mrs Sage — actress
and First Ever Aerial Female.

There was a teensy problem then.
Mr Lunardi had been
too much the gentleman
to enquire how much I weighed,
so had miscalculated.
Gallantly, he exited the basket,
leaving it light enough to rise
and leaving me and the lovely
rich young man
to soar without him.

I had to get down on all fours
to do up the gondola's lacing
so I'm afraid the people of Piccadilly
had a view of my large

but rather delectable bottom.
Lord knows what they thought
I was doing, and gorgeous George,
(we were on first name terms by then)
did get rather overwrought —
I couldn't help but notice.
Then of course I trod
on the barometer,
so we couldn't actually tell
what heights we'd reached,

but other than that, well
we had a simply wonderful time.
We had Italian sparkling wine
and cold chicken
and called to the people below
though a speaking trumpet.

The views were magnificent
and I had no need whatsoever
of my smelling salts.

We landed at Harrow on the Hill
in an unharvested hayfield, unfortunately,
the farmer was a complete savage,
yelling and swearing most inappropriately
and accusing us of ruining his crop.
Thankfully we were rescued
by a delightful young gentleman
from Harrow School
who, as I'd hurt a tendon in my foot,
carried me to the local tavern
where we all got wonderfully drunk.

I did hear that in Mr Biggin's London Club
there was a deal of speculation
as to what else we might have engaged in
up there in the heavens; cries of
Did he board her? There's men for you.

I suppose that when I go out now
I shall be much looked at,

as if a native of the Aerial Regions
had come down to pay an earthly visit.

HOW TO MAKE A PIG-FACED WOMAN

First start a rumour, such as that started
about poor wealthy Gizel Steevans of Dublin; pious
and charitable, she paid for the building of a hospital,
but also wore a veil and was of a retiring disposition.

Then write a pamphlet — *A True Description*
of the Young Lady Born with the Face of a Pig.
Bind the slim volume in pigskin for special effect.
Put on show the silver trough from which she eats her gruel.

Next procure a black bear and drug with warm strong ale.
Shave its snout, neck, paws; lug to a comfortable chair
and dress in a lady's costume with padded bosom, frills
          and ribbons.
Satin gloves for the front paws, elegant shoes for the rear,
a large wig, blonde and ringletted, a fashionable hat on top.

Are you the heiress to a large fortune? Poke. *Grunt.*
Do you feed from a silver trough? Poke. *Grunt.*

Poor rich Gizel, horrified that the populace of Dublin
had turned her into a Pig Faced Woman — boys grunting
at her in the street, men jumping on the footstep of her carriage
to catch a glimpse of her snout — sat out on her balcony
with her perfectly ordinary face in full view and had her portrait
painted and hung in the hospital halls. To no avail.
Everyone knew Madame Steevans had the face of a pig.

BECAUSE YOU'RE WORTH IT CIRCA 1772

> *Fashion is infinitely superior to merit.*
> — Josiah Wedgwood

Even as a child I had beautiful hands,
not pudgy like my older sister's, whose fingers
couldn't stretch past half an octave on the piano keys.
My fingers are long and slender and elegant,
the perfect setting for the jewelled rings
my husband has bought and given to me.
I see him watch their gracefulness, my hands
and wrists, as I move them to smooth my skirts,
undo a button, or let down my hair.

Sometimes I catch a glimpse of cook's hands,
fingers like half boiled sausages, lumpen
and misshapen: or the parlourmaid's, red
and chapped, so rough it makes me feel quite ill.
I shudder even thinking about hands like those.
I couldn't bear to live with hands like those.

This year's new product, an arsenic mixture
specifically for hands, to whiten them,
was recommended to me by a friend.
I use it every day and it is marvellously
efficacious ; my hands grow paler by the week,

and then, in Mr Wedgewood's showroom,
Portland Lane, I see the most divine new range
of tea sets, specifically designed to complement
the whiteness of a lady's hands. I had to have one.
Now, when visitors call, the teapot's basalt blackness

allows me to show the beauty of my alabaster fingers
to wonderful effect. I see them look —
though lately I have felt lethargic, a little nauseous,
with stomach cramps and in all honesty
not enjoying company as much as once I did:
I do hope I am not becoming ill.

SABRINA

There is absolutely no need to feel sorry for me,
it worked out very well; I became Mrs Bicknell,
and John was a good man — not that Mr Day wasn't,

strange yes, with his philosophy and notions, and yes,
a bit cruel when you look at it from the point of view
of a twelve year old girl,
which is what I was when he picked me,

still he kept his word and without him
I might have ended up on the streets; most likely would,
for what else could I have done, an orphan with no one.

I sense your disapproval: well, maybe you live
in different times and there are no poor children
to be exploited, no small boys are crippled
by being sent up chimneys; no children
starve to death, no babies get left outside to die,

and no rich person could just arrive at a foundling hospital
to choose a little girl to take home with them,
to do with what they wish, but that's how it was
when I lived and it could have been worse for me.
It can always be worse.

Mr Day was a disciple of Rousseau, and too deeply earnest,
so they said, to submit to the ordinary compromises of society,
which was why he determined on his experiment
to train a girl to be the perfect wife: high virtued,
courageous, with a taste for literature, science and philosophy,
but with the simplest of tastes in clothes, food and way of life.
She should be prepared to live calmly, in seclusion, and in total

obedience to her husband. Of course I knew nothing of this
the day they lined up us girls, the ones just approaching
     womanhood,
but still innocent, and he walked up and down, looking at us.

He stopped in front of me and I looked up from below my eyelids,
saw a tall man, heavy jawed with a tangle of dark hair.
This child seems suitable, he said in his clear voice. Later,
after he'd taught me to read, I used to think he talked like a book,
but on that day I took in little of his fancy words, before I
knew it
I was parcelled up and put onto the coach with him, lurching
through the dark, cold and afraid, Shrewsbury to London,
where he picked another girl, dark-haired, a nice contrast
to my own flaxen locks, but the same age as me. Two of us,
twice the chance for success. He named her Lucretia: me
he called Sabrina, and that's what I've been known as ever since.

I was so sick on the ship to France I thought
I was like to die: and wanted to.
By the time we got to Avignon I hated her
with her constant whining and complaining
and always trying to get me into trouble.

He did his best to educate us
in the severest of principles
so that we would acquire
the strength of mind he required
in a wife. We were wild little things
though, fought and scrapped,
biting and kicking and hair pulling.
At least I learnt to read, not like her
who couldn't even do that.

By the time we moved back to England
he'd given up on her, called her
invincibly stupid, which she was,

but good to his word he placed her
with a milliner as an apprentice.
I heard she married a linen draper,
so she did all right too, I told you
he wasn't a bad man. He kept on
with me, trying to shape me
to his satisfaction, and not succeeding.
When he dropped melted sealing wax
onto my arm, I just couldn't keep quiet,
I squealed, and pulled my arm away.
When he fired pistols round my feet
and at my petticoats, I have to confess
I screamed, and cursed him; when
he tested my reticence, I found
I couldn't keep a secret either, so that
was that, I was out of the running
to be his wife and sent to boarding school.
He was a good man, he could have
just turned me out onto the streets.

I heard the woman he did marry,
Esther, when he made her walk
barefoot in the snow, wept
but did not complain, and that
is what he appears to have wanted.

I was sorry enough when I heard he had died.
Trying to break the spirit of a horse
it threw him on his head.

BRUISING PEG

At Hockey in the Hole, or in the Amphitheatre
where cocks and bulls and Irish women fight
I fought

the vendor of sprats from Billingsgate,
the ass driver from Stoke Newington,
the Newgate Market basket woman
the Hibernian Heroine
the Championess of the City

and I pulverised them all: my physical capital
no less than any man's. I am weapon and target,
bare-knuckled, bare-breasted, my hair tied up,
half pint of gin in me, I fear nothing and no one.
Let the bets be laid and the blood begin.

JOLLY DAISY

We were having a hard season, wet weekends,
cold winds, and farmers too worried 'bout their crops
to go to carnival; worst of all, we didn't have a freak.
We'd a good enough show. I did a bit of fire eating
and sword swallowing, Krinko hammered nails
up his nose, Captain Billy did the Bed of Pain
and the Human Ostrich swallowed mice, brought
them up again still wriggling: all the kind of stuff
anyone would enjoy, but we badly needed a freak.

The night I first saw Jolly Daisy, she staggered in
wheezing and puffing, her fluffy pink dress soaked
with sweat, her thick legs barely able to support
the great mass of her body. Well, I thought,
it's not the original Siamese twins but it'll do.

Leave me lie down.

Three of us supported her to the bed,
where she collapsed, a mountain of exhausted flesh.
The four legs of the bed sank into the wet earth of the top.
Her dress had ridden up over her vast thighs.

I think I'm dying,
this time I'm dying for sure.

We had our freak.

*

Me and him, the fire eater,
we get to talking between shows.

91

I show him a picture of my kid.
You have a child, *all surprised,*
Is she…? *No I tells him,*
she ain't fat like me, she's normal.
It ain't wise though
for her to know that I'm her mother.
The nuns send me pictures.

Men ain't no good.
I'd be a faithful wife
to a decent man:, sure a wife
ought to help her husband some,
but sometimes he ought
to make some money for hisself.
The one I left to come here,
I have to give him due,
he was a good talker.
A good talker
can point an act up nicely,
 he used to get fifteen
minutes of comedy out of me —
like he'd drop a coin,
tell me to pick it up
and when I bend over,
my skirt rides up so high
it shows my arse, that
gives the crowd a laugh.
Krinko just says — **This
is Jolly Daisy
the fattest lady in the world** —
and the tip looks and passes by.

I'll stay till the end of the season,
then move on
to one of the big city's dime museums.

VIOLET

OF DAISY AND VIOLET
THE FABULOUS CO-JOINED HILTON SISTERS
1908 - 1969

Us is I are Kate Skinner's
unwanted bastard horror,
sold to the midwife,
displayed, alongside
the Rose's Royal Midgets
for your entertainment.

Auntie Lou and Sir beat *her*,
and beat me; teach *us* to sing
and dance, and *us* dance and sing
all over the place, Germany,
Australia, the USA

then Edith and her carnival
balloon man Myer owns *us*
and *us* lives with them
in a fancy house designed
by Frank Lloyd Wright
cause *us* is very famous
everybody wants to talk
to *us*, everybody loves *us*.
It's only spoiled by *her*,
like when Bob Hope
asks me to dance
and *her* tags along
spoiling the steps,
or when I sleep with William
and *her* doesn't like it, cries.

I'm very popular — Blue Steel,
his lovely musician's fingers,
Harry Mason, with his battered
boxer's face and strong arms,
Don Galvan who plays me
tunes on his guitar,
and Maurice Lambert,
my lovely band leader —
who wants to marry me
not *her* or *us*

and *hers*, Jack Lewis, too shy
to marry *her us,*

so twenty one States
turn me and Maurice down
on moral grounds,
because of *her us.*

Permanently single
permanently double

then Harry teaches me
how to use my mind
and sometimes I can do it,
become a great escapologist
like him, escape from *her* and *us.*

Us escapes from Edith too,
 us is legally free.
I can drink cocktails
and spend *us* money
as I please whether *her*
likes it or not

though still, *us* is show
business, *us* is Freaks,

then *us* is out of fashion,
run out on by our rat of an agent, abandoned
in Charlotte, North Carolina, I find *us* work.
Me and *her* sell hotdogs, but it doesn't work out;
other vendors, they don't like that me and *her*
are stealing their business by being *us*
.

so me and *her* sell groceries in Charlie's Park-
n-Shop, live in a house owned by the church.
The dress *dress* that Charlie has made for me
and *us* and the way *us* stand behind the counter —
some people don't even realise that me
and *her* am *us*.

Hong Kong flu takes *her*
me *us*, they find *us*
on top of the heating grille.
It was *her* who died first: me
alone at last with myself
without myself, *us*.

HOW TO SWALLOW A SWORD

There are over two hundred names
in the Sword Swallowers' Hall of Fame
and that's not counting the fakirs,
the Greeks and Romans, the Mayan Indians,
the Chinese, the Japanese or the Sufis.

There is Signor Wandana, Professor Pierce,
the Mighty Ajax, Chief Willie Bowlegs,
The Great Zadma, Skippy the Clown
and Edith Clifford — Champion
Sword Swallower of the World,
taught the skill at thirteen
by one-legged Delmo Fritz.

begin with something short
a pair of scissors
or a paper knife
learn to control
your gag reflex that involuntary
reaction that arises in the nerves

keep a bowl beside you
until you have conditioned yourself
to do what your defence mechanisms
try to prohibit

teach your upper gastro-
intestinal tract to relax
tilt your head back
extend the neck
align the mouth
with the oesophagus

move the tongue aside
line up the sword
and move it
through the mouth
pharynx past
the sphincter muscle

on its way down
the sword straightens out
oesophageal curves
nudges the heart aside
enters the stomach.

Edith, employed by Barnun and Bailey,
was feted in the Royal Courts of Europe
(Houdini said) for her more than ordinary
personal charms, her refined taste in clothes
and her unswerving devotion to her art.

Blades of twenty inches
without a problem, sometimes ten
or sixteen at a time.

Two marriages,
Thomas, the Elastic Stretch Man
and after him, Karl the Trapeze Artist,
then retirement, to open her grocery store.

Her grandson does not remember her
ever speaking of her showbusiness career
and never saw her swallow a sword,
though he has kept one in a cupboard at his home
and can be persuaded to pose with it for the camera.

YOUTH RIDING

after Picasso

I will both remember and forget
how easy it is and how light I am;
the smell of the trodden earth
in the big ring, sweat and perfume
of the crowd. It was never just an act.
See me, my hair flowing behind me,
my body obliviously balanced
on the moment's broad back.

NIETZSCHE'S HORSE

Sympathy is no contemptible choice,
and true or not, the story haunts me,
Turin, Piazzo Carlo Alberto,
the adult self
transformed
to the child self
and weeping over the beaten horse.

Sing me a new song. The world is trans-
formed and all the Heavens sing for joy.

DISSOLUTION OF THE CIRCUS

After the last of the big cats died
toothless and emaciated, the elephant
was impounded by animal welfare
and the ponies were sold to a riding school
where they soon forgot all their tricks.
The bearded lady had electrolysis,
married the fat man, who'd joined a gym
and was less than half the man he used to be.
The clown enrolled with the Open University
— English Literature and Philosophy —
and the contortionist gave up cocaine,
finally straightened out his head.
There's only the two of us left now,
me and the ring master with his top hat
and his whip and though the spangles
have mostly fallen off my costume
I can still balance up there on the wire.